Giving expression
to the events that
punctuate life . . .

With love

To:

Cecile

From:

Mary (and Marvin)

Date:

May 16. 2010

YOU are a success in yourself!
    Happy Birthday
        and many more

celebrations for the successes of life

WOW

HOWARD
PUBLISHING CO.

Martha Bolton

the exclamat!on series

Our purpose at Howard Publishing is to:
• *Increase faith* in the hearts of growing Christians
• *Inspire holiness* in the lives of believers
• *Instill hope* in the hearts of struggling people everywhere
Because He's coming again!

Wow! © 2006 by Martha Bolton
All rights reserved. Printed in the United States of America
Published by Howard Publishing Co., Inc.
3117 North Seventh Street, West Monroe, LA 71291-2227
www.howardpublishing.com

06 07 08 09 10 11 12 13 14 15   10 9 8 7 6 5 4 3 2 1

Edited by Between the Lines
Interior design by Stephanie D. Walker and Tennille Paden
Illustrations by Rex Bohn

Library of Congress Cataloging-in-Publication Data

Wow! : humor for the lighter side of life / [compiled by] Martha Bolton.
    p. cm.— (The exclamation series)
  ISBN 1-58229-478-X
  1. Quotations, English. 2. Wit and humor. I. Bolton, Martha, 1951-II. Series.
PN6084.H8W69 2005
082'.02'07—dc22

                                                     2005052571

Scripture quotations are taken from the *Holy Bible, New International Version.*®
Copyright © 1973, 1978, 1984 by International Bible Society. Used by permission
of Zondervan Publishing House. All rights reserved.

Contents

Contents

WOW!

Where would we be without our *Wow!* days? We need those special occasions and events that remind us of our significance (birthdays), our love (weddings and anniversaries), and our commitment and dedication to service (retirements, tributes, honors, and awards).

Where would the world be without the *Wow!* people? The people who believed when others doubted? The people who hung in there when others quit? The people who said, "I know I can" when others said, "I'm not even going to try."

Introduction

This book is about celebrating the *Wow!* moments and the *Wow!* people in our lives. It's about joy, validation, romance, remembering, saluting, honoring, congratulating, thanking, and giving well-earned credit where credit is due. *Wow!*

Part One

WOW!

The *Wow!* of Special Moments

He who enjoys doing
and enjoys what he has done is happy.

Johann Wolfgang von Goethe

A *Wow!* moment can be an occasion such as a birthday, anniversary, retirement, wedding, birth of a baby, or any other special day. It's a time for celebration. It may be a special day to many, just a few, or perhaps it's special only to you. In any case, *Wow!* days add excitement to life. They're not just another day on the calendar. They're a day like no other. You will only have one twenty-first, thirty-fifth, seventieth, or whatever other number birthday you happen to be celebrating. (Some women have been known to have multiple twenty-ninth birthdays, but that's cheating.)

A *Wow!* can also be an accomplishment such as graduating, winning an award, opening a new business, buying a new home, signing a record deal, or some other memorable event.

Wow! days and events are to be remembered, cherished, and celebrated. They're milestone moments—some small, some great, but all worthy of recognition. So whether your *Wow!* is an occasion or an accomplishment, it's time to cheer. This is a day to say *Wow!*

Part One: *Wow!* Moments

You did it!
You beat the odds.
You climbed the heights.
You forged ahead.
You aimed your sites.
You struck pure gold.
You didn't quit.
You gave your all.
You did it!

You Did It!
The *Wow!* of Accomplishment

Always bear in mind that your own resolution to
succeed is more important than any other.

Abraham Lincoln

Success requires hard work, risk taking, perseverance,
and a whole lot of faith. Obviously, you have all those
qualities, or you wouldn't be where you are today. You
kept Going and didn't give up. You hung in there long
after less-committed people had thrown in the towel. You
believed in your mission in spite of the naysayers. You

stayed focused on your purpose and put forth your best effort.

Just think of all those hours you spent studying or practicing your craft to finally get to this moment. All the time you spent at the library or sitting in front of the computer. All the training and work you did to prepare for the big competition. You gave it your all and never looked back.

Whatever it took to make you the winner you are today was well worth it. Seeing all that you've accomplished, all we can say is . . . *Wow!*

Nothing in this world can take the place of
persistence. Talent will not; nothing is more
common than unsuccessful men with talent.
Genius will not; unrewarded genius
is almost a proverb. Education will not;
the world is full of educated derelicts.
Persistence, determination, and hard work
make the difference.

Calvin Coolidge

The roots of true achievement lie in the will to
become the best that you can become.

Harold Taylor

Congratulations Are in Order!

Commendable!
Outstanding!
Noteworthy!
Glorious!
Remarkable!
Admirable!
Terrific!
Unbelievable!
Laudable!
Amazing!
Tremendous!
Impressive!
Overwhelming!
Nice!
Superb!

It is time for us all to stand and cheer for the doer, the achiever—the one who recognizes the challenge and does something about it.

Vince Lombardi

The achievement of one goal
should be the starting point of another.

Alexander Graham Bell

Wonderful!

The *Wow!* of Good News

There is good news from Washington today.
Congress is deadlocked and can't act.

Will Rogers

Good news can arrive by letter, e-mail, phone call, or skywriting. It can even be written in the cap of a soda bottle. However it comes, it makes our day to hear it.

Good news that surprises us is exceptionally nice. Maybe it arrives on a day when everything else is going wrong. While we're sitting there wondering what else can go south, unexpected good news arrives, reenergizing our hope and bringing the smile back to our faces.

- "We've taken another look at those x-rays, and we're not going to have to operate after all."

- "Sorry, I guess we made a mistake in our calculations. You only owe $12, not $12,000."

- "I've checked out your television—it doesn't need a new control panel. It just needed to be plugged in."

Good news isn't always unexpected—sometimes it's preceded by plenty of anticipation. You know you've been nominated for an award or that you've applied to the university and are waiting for word on your admission status. You bought that soda knowing that inside the cap it either says "Winner!" or "Sorry, try again." Or you entered a contest, and your heart pounds as you await the final tally of the judges' votes. No matter how many times you may have lost in the past, this time you know things could be different. This time it just might happen. This time you might just hear . . .

- "We're happy to tell you that your oil painting received first place in the art show!"

- "The board has met, and we've decided you would be the best candidate for the position."

- "We are writing to inform you that you have been accepted into our university."

- "The votes are in, and you're elected!"

Good news, whatever it is and however it comes, deserves a *Wow!*

Part One: *Wow!* Moments

Everyone has inside of him
a piece of good news.
The good news is that you
don't know how great you can be!
How much you can love!
What you can accomplish!
And what your potential is!

Anne Frank

Happy Day!

The *Wow!* of Special Days

Our hearts are so full that we must celebrate.

Liberty Hyde Bailey

Life is full of *Wow!* days: birthdays, graduations, weddings, anniversaries, retirements—days that deserve to be celebrated.

September 1 and September 2 may not mean anything to you, but they mean something to me. They are my birthdays.

Yes, I have two. For eighteen years I thought my birthday was September 2, but when I sent away for my birth certificate at age eighteen, I discovered that I was really born on the first day of the month. And no, it wasn't because I came into the world at midnight. I was born at 10 a.m. So almost a whole day of my life is unaccounted for! Maybe I was busy plotting my escape from the hospital. Whatever the reason, I've forgiven my parents for forgetting the day I was born. I was the last of five kids, so by then they were probably just too tired to keep track!

My wedding anniversary is another day I honor. Neither my husband nor I have ever forgotten our anniversary. Even in the lean years when we couldn't celebrate the way we would have liked to, we still tried to make it special (like going *inside* at McDonald's instead of just ordering in the drive-through lane).

My husband remembers the date of his graduation from the Los Angeles Police Academy. He also remembers when he retired. All three retirement dates. I'm reasonably certain that he holds the record for having retired the most times from the LAPD.

I'm sure you have your own list of *Wow!* days. Whether you've memorized them, written them in your date book, or programmed them into your palm pilot, you know them. They're your special days, and they're worth celebrating!

The *Wow!* of Birthdays

Birthdays mean you've made it another year! No matter what you've had to endure, you're still here. You have reached this point and, as my mother used to say, "the good Lord willing and the creek don't rise," you've got plenty more to look forward to.

Birthdays are a celebration of you, from the moment you took your very first breath to the moment you read these words. It doesn't matter whether a crowd of people has gathered to celebrate your existence or it's just a party of one—your birthday is definitely a *Wow!* day.

Your birthday is a special time to celebrate
the gift of "you" to the world.

Unknown

Part One: *Wow!* Moments

Women are most fascinating between the ages
of thirty-five and forty, after they have won a
few races and know how to pace themselves.
Since few women ever pass forty, maximum
fascination can continue indefinitely.

Christian Dior

To be seventy years young
is sometimes far more cheerful and hopeful
than to be forty years old.

Oliver Wendell Holmes Jr.

The most effective way to remember
your wife's birthday is to forget it once.

Unknown

The *Wow!* of Graduations

You made it! Whether it's middle school, high school, beauty school, law school, medical school, or any other school, you did it! You put in the study time, you passed all the necessary tests, and you graduated. That's no small feat. In some cases, though, it might be a small miracle!

Graduates, your families are probably very proud of you right now. They weren't altogether confident that you would ever make it through potty training; so you can't begin to imagine the enormity of their sense of relief today. Without question, today would be an extremely opportune time to ask for money.

Gary Bolding

There is a good reason they call these
ceremonies "commencement exercises."
Graduation is not the end; it's the beginning.

Orrin Hatch

You are educated.
Your certification is in your degree.
You may think of it as the ticket to the good life.
Let me ask you to think of an alternative.
Think of it as your ticket to change the world.

Tom Brokaw

The *Wow!* of Weddings

You see him standing at the altar as you walk through the chapel door and begin your walk down the aisle. He has never looked more handsome. When he sees you, tears form in his eyes. He has always known you're beautiful, but he's never seen you this radiant.

Or maybe you're both planning to go before a justice of the peace and share your vows in a small, personal ceremony.

However long you've been dating, however you first met—whether you saw each other from across a crowded room, bumped carts in the vegetable aisle at the local grocery store, shared a pew at church, or sat side by side on a bench at a football game—wherever and whenever it was that your hearts first connected, you have now decided to make a commitment to each other in marriage, and that's a definite *Wow!*

celebrations for the successes of life

A happy marriage
is the union of two good forgivers.

Ruth Bell Graham

What greater thing is there for two human souls
than to feel that they are joined . . .
to strengthen each other . . . to be at one
with each other in silent unspeakable memories.

George Eliot

Marriage is an alliance entered into by a man who can't sleep with the window shut, and a woman who can't sleep with the window open.

George Bernard Shaw

The *Wow!* of Anniversaries

Some of us have been at this thing called marriage for a while now. We've matured in our love enough to know that there is no perfect marriage. If you think your marriage is perfect, you're probably still at your reception. In all marriages there will be ups and downs, a good amount of give and take, wonderful moments you will cherish forever, and moments when you will wonder what in the world you were thinking when you took that vow. Marriage is a process of learning to coexist. That's difficult for neighbors, coworkers, and even countries to do; what makes us think it won't require a little extra work for lovers to pull it off (especially if they're complete opposites)?

Someone once said that a good rule to follow is to never go to bed angry. I agree with that rule. I'm going on my third week without sleep.

Seriously, though, remaining husband and wife through thick and thin, good and bad, ups and downs is worthy of celebration. Anniversaries are definitely *Wow!* days.

For two people in a marriage to live together day after day is unquestionably the one miracle the Vatican has overlooked.

Bill Cosby

More marriages might survive
if the partners realized that sometimes the better comes after the worse.

Doug Larson

A wedding anniversary is the celebration of love, trust, partnership, tolerance and tenacity.
The order varies for any given year.

Paul Sweeney

Grow old with me!
The best is yet to be.

Robert Browning

I love being married.
It's so great to find that one special person
you want to annoy for the rest of your life.

Rita Rudner

Part One: *Wow!* Moments

The *Wow!* of Retirement

You've proven yourself to be a dedicated worker. You put in your time. You were dependable, trustworthy, a team player. You took pride in your work, and now it's finally time to rest on your laurels. Or start another career. That's the nice thing about retirement—the choice of how to spend your days is all yours.

Don't underestimate the value of doing nothing, of just going along, listening to all the things you can't hear, and not bothering.

A. A. Milne

The best time to start thinking about your retirement is before the boss does.

Unknown

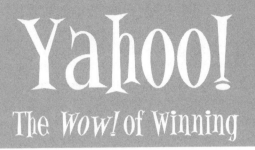

Yahoo!

The *Wow!* of Winning

Winners have simply formed the habit of doing things losers don't like to do.

Albert Gray

It doesn't matter whether you've just won a Pulitzer Prize or a coloring contest, the Nobel Peace Prize or the Publisher's Clearing House Sweepstakes, an Academy Award or a bag of French fries from your favorite fast-food restaurant. The important thing is that you're a winner! You are to be congratulated.

Your shining moment may have been marked by a

plaque, a trophy, or a certificate. Perhaps it was written about in newspapers or talked about on radio and television. Or maybe just a handful of family and friends are aware of your accomplishment. It doesn't matter. What does matter is that you've been deemed a winner, and regardless of who else knows it, you deserve to celebrate!

I'm a winner each
and every time I go into the ring.

George Foreman

The winners in life think constantly
in terms of I can, I will, and I am.
Losers, on the other hand,
concentrate their waking thoughts
on what they should have or would have done,
or what they can't do.

Denis Waitley

Way to Go!

The *Wow!* of Honors

The quality of a person's life is in direct proportion to their commitment to excellence, regardless of their chosen field of endeavor.

Vince Lombardi

Comedian Bob Hope knew what it was like to be honored. He's listed in *Guinness World Records* as "the world's most honored entertainer." He has been presented with awards, trophies, plaques, honorary degrees, statues, keys to who knows how many cities, medals, and more. Maybe that's why he kept putting additions on his house—he needed more room to store them all! When President Kennedy presented him with the Congressional Gold Medal in 1963, Bob said, "I feel very

humble, but I think I have the strength of character to fight it."

Even if we haven't obtained world-record status, it still feels nice to be honored. It validates our efforts and our talents. You, too, are being recognized for your excellent accomplishments. You are the best of the best. You're a *Wow!*

Desire is the key to motivation, but it's determination and commitment to an unrelenting pursuit of your goal—a commitment to excellence—that will enable you to attain the success you seek.

Mario Andretti

Make it a life-rule to give your best to whatever
passes through your hands.

Orison Swett Marden

We are what we repeatedly do.
Excellence, then, is a habit.

Socrates

You da Man!

The *Wow!* of Amazing Feats

It had long since come to my attention that people of accomplishment rarely sat back and let things happen to them. They went out and happened to things.

Leonardo da Vinci

Former president George H. W. Bush wanted to celebrate his seventy-fifth birthday in a unique way. He wanted it to be memorable. Exhilarating. Fun. So he went skydiving.

He even repeated the feat five years later for his eightieth birthday, parachuting down some thirteen thousand feet above his presidential library. Some eighty-year-olds might have found all the excitement they needed just blowing out their birthday candles. But George Herbert Walker Bush wanted to celebrate with a *Wow!*

An amazing feat can also be something we do for others. In dire emergencies mothers have been known to lift the weight of a car to save a child trapped beneath it. Dads and moms have worked two, sometimes even three, jobs to enable their sons or daughters to attend their college of choice. Researchers have labored for years, sometimes without remuneration, to discover cures for diseases. Missionaries, soldiers, law-enforcement officers, firefighters, teachers, and others have paid the ultimate price when they lost their lives in the course of their duties.

All are amazing feats done by amazing people—and you are one of them. *Wow!*

Courage is not the absence of fear, but rather the judgment that something else is more important than fear.

Ambrose Redmoon

It is not the critic who counts, nor the person who points out how the strong person stumbled or where the doer of deeds could have done better. The credit belongs to the person who is actually in the arena; whose face is actually marred by dust and sweat and blood, who strives valiantly, who errs and comes short again and again, who knows great enthusiasm and great devotion, whose life is spent in a worthy cause; who, at best, knows in the end the triumph of high achievement and at worst, if failure wins out, it at least wins with greatness, so that this person's place shall never be with those timid souls who know neither victory nor defeat.

Theodore Roosevelt

I tell you the truth, if you have faith as small as a mustard seed, you can say to this mountain, "Move from here to there" and it will move. Nothing will be impossible for you.

Matthew 17:20

It is not because things are difficult
that we do not dare, it is because
we do not dare that they are difficult.

Seneca

High Five!

The *Wow!* of Success

> Desire is the starting point of all achievement, not a hope, not a wish, but a keen, pulsating desire which transcends everything.
>
> Napoleon Hill

Ask any successful person, and most will tell you that something deep inside told them they could achieve their dreams if only they would follow them. These people may not have even known their primary colors yet, but in their minds they envisioned themselves painting masterpieces. Maybe the only song they could play on the piano was "Chopsticks," but in their heads they envisioned sold-out concerts with standing ovations. An inherent drive pushed them to succeed.

They had an internal coach encouraging them to keep going, to learn their craft, to do the work, to be the best they could be—and if they would, the rest would soon follow. And so they did—you did—and what followed was the *Wow!* of success.

Look at a day when you are supremely satisfied at the end. It's not a day when you lounge around doing nothing; it's when you've had everything to do and you've done it.

Margaret Thatcher

Ask yourself the secret of *your* success. Listen to your answer, and practice it.

Richard Bach

You Made It!

The *Wow!* of Overcoming Obstacles

I have learned that success is to be measured not so much by the position that one has reached in life as by the obstacles which he has had to overcome while trying to succeed.

Booker T. Washington

It's difficult enough to achieve *Wow!* status with procrastination, doubt, fear, and negative attitudes getting in the way. But some achievers have had to face even greater obstacles than these. They've had to overcome physical, economic, emotional, and other challenges.

Well-meaning friends and family members may have told them not to set their sights so high, reminding them of their limitations instead of pointing out the many possibilities. Perhaps others told them their goals were too ambitious, impossible for them to reach—that they should just let them go or at least bring them down to a more manageable size.

But lucky for the world, these brave souls went ahead and pursued their dreams. They ended up doing what others said they couldn't do. Helen Keller and Ray Charles accomplished more and could "see" more about life than many sighted people. And can you imagine anyone telling Grandma Moses or Mother Teresa that they were too old to accomplish anything significant? Abraham Lincoln didn't let his family's financial constraints restrict his ambition. He read law books by the light of a fire in the fireplace. Franklin Delano Roosevelt is another president who didn't let obstacles stand in his way. He had polio and, so far, has been the only wheelchair-bound president of the United States. James Earl Jones overcame a speech impediment as a young child to become one of the most impressive voices in Hollywood.

The list goes on and on. Sometimes *Wow!* people have to overcome overwhelming obstacles, but they do it. Not only do they live out their dreams; often they make history in the process.

Part One: *Wow!* Moments

The greater the obstacle,
the more glory in overcoming it.

Jean Baptiste Poquelin Molière

Obstacles are those frightful things you see
when you take your eyes off your goal.

Henry Ford

Nothing splendid has ever been achieved except
by those who dared believe that something
inside of them was superior to circumstances.

Bruce Barton

Accept the challenges
so that you may feel the exhilaration of victory.

George S. Patton

Hang On!
The *Wow!* of Perseverance

Every great work, every big accomplishment,
has been brought into manifestation through
holding to the vision, and often
just before the big achievement,
comes apparent failure and discouragement.

Florence Scovel Shinn

Whatever you've achieved in life, no doubt perseverance
played a major role. Without the will to keep on going
in the face of failure, to ignore the doubters and believe
in yourself, to go up against seemingly insurmountable

odds, to hang in there when the easier thing would have been to quit, very little in this world would ever get accomplished. But not everyone has perseverance, and that's what makes you a *Wow!*

Perseverance is what makes you say, "Maybe next time" when others are saying, "This is never going to work." It's what keeps you pressing ahead after everyone else has given up. It's what enables you to say, "I can," when everyone around you is saying, "Are you crazy? You'll never do it in a million years!"

Perseverance means you believe in yourself—not that you'll never fail but that you won't give up until you've exhausted every viable option. And even then you just might keep on trying. That's the *Wow!* kind of perseverance.

Pay no attention to what the critics say . . .
Remember, a statue has never been set up in
honor of a critic!

Jean Sibelius

All achievement is the triumph of persistence.

John Rennie

Most people give up just when they're about to achieve success. They quit on the one-yard line. They give up at the last minute of the game, one foot from a winning touchdown.

H. Ross Perot

Persistent people begin their success where others end in failure.

Edward Eggleston

Perseverance is a great element of success.
If you only knock long enough and loud enough
at the gate, you are sure to wake up somebody.

Henry Wadsworth Longfellow

Success is not final, failure is not fatal: it is the
courage to continue that counts.

Winston Churchill

Good for You!

The *Wow!* of Getting Up Again

No man ever achieved worthwhile success
who did not, at one time or other,
find himself with at least one foot hanging
well over the brink of failure.

Napoleon Hill

Most people don't arrive at a place of success without failing once or twice along the way. Or maybe ten or twenty times. Or thousands, as Michael Jordan once confessed: "I've missed more than nine thousand shots in my career. I've lost almost three hundred games. Twenty-six times I've been trusted to take the game-winning shot and missed. I've failed over and over and over again in my life. And that is why I succeed."

Success often travels on the back of failure. Did you know that Walt Disney's first cartoon company went bankrupt? If he had given up, where would we spend our Disney dollars? Thomas Edison tried hundreds of different ways to invent the light bulb and failed. Thankfully, he tried one more way. Barbra Streisand's stage debut was in a show that opened and closed the same night. At just nineteen years of age, she easily could have decided to sell insurance—a fine career, but look what the world would have missed out on musically.

Defeat, failure, rejection, loss—don't dwell on them, but do remember them. Once success comes, they make great anecdotes. In the meantime, when you fall, get up and try again. You never know when the next attempt will make you a *Wow!*

Part One: *Wow!* Moments

It takes twenty years
to become an overnight success.

Eddie Cantor

Success is how high you
bounce when you hit bottom.

George S. Patton

Never let the fear of striking out
get in your way.

Babe Ruth

I couldn't wait for success,
so I went ahead without it.

Jonathan Winters

So?

So you failed?
   Get up and start over.
So you lost your way?
   Go back and find it.
So you were rejected?
   It doesn't change your worth.
So you slipped up?
   Regain your footing and keep
   on going.
So you were defeated?
   One battle is not the war.
So you got off track?
   Get back on it.
So you hit bottom?
   Turn around and head back up
   to the top.

Supposing you have tried and failed again and again. You may have a fresh start any moment you choose, for this thing we call "failure" is not the falling down, but the staying down.

Mary Pickford

Ever tried? Ever failed? No matter.
Try again. Fail again. Fail better.

Samuel Beckett

Part One: *Wow!* Moments

Never confuse a single defeat with a final defeat.

F. Scott Fitzgerald

Notice the difference between what happens
when a man says to himself,
"I have failed three times" and what happens
when he says, "I am a failure."

S. I. Hayakawa

Oh Me!
The *Wow!* of Discovering Yourself

Sometimes you find yourself in the middle
of nowhere, and sometimes in the middle of
nowhere you find yourself.

Unknown

There's someone very important I hope you get to meet someday. Yourself.

So many of us go through life never really knowing who we are. We get excited whenever we meet a celebrity. When we meet the person with whom we want to spend the rest of our lives, we're walking on air. The first time we hold our children, we don't think anyone else could be that special. We meet friends, bosses, and perfect strangers, but some of us will live our entire lives and never meet the one person we should know best—ourselves.

Take a few minutes to fill in the answers to the questions on the next pages. I hope after you do, you'll find that you're a pretty awesome person after all. You may even discover a few things that make you say *Wow!*

Pleased to Meet You!

- Who are you?

- What do you need?

- What is your passion?

- What events in your past (both positive and negative) have made you who you are today?

- What will you regret not having done when you reach the end of your life?

- What accomplishments are you most proud of?

- What about yourself do you wish you could change?

- What about yourself do you wish you could laugh about?

- Who has been the most influential person in your life?

- If your life had a mission statement, what would it be?

Part One: *Wow!* Moments

- What do you wish your life had more of? Less of?

- What do you believe you could accomplish if given a chance?

- What holds you back?

- What do you fear most?

- What are your strengths?

- What are your weaknesses?

- If you had to write a tribute to yourself and you weren't allowed to say anything negative, what would you write?

Be yourself; no base imitator of another,
but your best self.
There is something which you can do better
than another. Listen to the inward voice
and bravely obey that.
Do the things at which you are great,
not what you were never made for.

Ralph Waldo Emerson

Part One: *Wow!* Moments

We all have a calling. We all have a purpose
in life. Not all of us are meant to be artists
who paint on canvases, but we all have a gift.
Sometimes it is presented to us early in our
lives, and other times we realize our special gifts
later, when we least expect.

Mark Victor Hansen

God has given each of us our "marching
orders." Our purpose here on Earth is to find
those orders and carry them out. Those orders
acknowledge our special gifts.

Søren Kierkegaard

Think positively about yourself . . .
Ask God who made you
to keep on remaking you.

Norman Vincent Peale

Part One: *Wow!* Moments

I've always known I was gifted, which is not the easiest thing in the world for a person to know, because you're not responsible for your gift, only for what you do with it.

Hazel Scott

The lesson that stands out for me is that true nobility is not about being better than anyone else—it's about being better than you used to be.

Wayne Dyer

Each of us has a fire in our heart
for something.
It's our goal in life
to find it and to keep it lit.

Mary Lou Retton

Part One: *Wow!* Moments

Let your light shine before men, that they
may see your good deeds and praise your
Father in heaven.

Matthew 5:16

Part Two

How to Be a Wow!

Be a *Wow!*

You are not here merely to make a living.
You are here in order to enable the world to live
more amply, with greater vision, with a finer spirit
of hope and achievement. You are here
to enrich the world, and you impoverish yourself
if you forget the errand.

Woodrow Wilson

Besides an occasion, a *Wow!* can also be a person. Some people are walking, talking *Wows!* These people can't help but make a positive difference in the world. They possess and exhibit *Wow!* qualities, such as perseverance, dedication, a drive to succeed, confidence, and so much more. *Wow!* people don't let failure, doubt, discouragement, obstacles, or fear stand in their way. They know who they are and what they want out of life. They adapt when they need to and stand fast when they must.

A *Wow!* person can be a president or a postal worker, a truck driver or a CEO, a lawyer or a stay-at-home mom or dad. *Wow!* people come in all shapes and sizes, all nationalities, and from all economic and religious backgrounds. The one thing they have in common is that they've made the world a better place by being part of it.

To follow, without halt, one aim:
there's the secret of success.

Anna Pavlova

You are a *Wow!*
You've got what it takes,
and we celebrate you!

Oh Boy!

Wow! = Enthusiasm

Those who are fired with an enthusiastic idea
and who allow it to take hold and dominate their
thoughts find that new worlds open for them.
As long as enthusiasm holds out,
so will new opportunities.

Norman Vincent Peale

WALKIES?

Have you ever met people who, no matter what they're
working on, seem to bubble over with enthusiasm? It's
like they are their own personal cheerleading squad. They
refuse to get discouraged, no matter how many things go

wrong. They believe so much in what they're doing that nothing deters them. These folks are eternal optimists, enthusiastic down to the bone, and they refuse to give in to negativism.

Wow! people are all this and more. They bring enthusiasm to a whole new level, and their enthusiasm is the contagious kind. You can't be around a *Wow!* without having some of his or her enthusiasm spill over onto you. Before you know it, you're agreeing with his or her vision and asking what you can do to help. Enthusiasm is an important part of being a *Wow!*

Don't ask yourself what the world needs;
ask yourself what makes you come alive.
And then go and do that.
Because what the world needs
is people who have come alive.

Harold Whitman

The real secret of success is enthusiasm.

Walter Chrysler

Part Two: How to Be a *Wow!*

Nothing great was ever achieved
without enthusiasm.

Ralph Waldo Emerson

None are so old as those
who have outlived enthusiasm.

Henry David Thoreau

All we need to make us really happy is
something to be enthusiastic about.

Charles Kingsley

I Dare You!

Wow! = Daring

Every really new idea looks crazy at first.

Alfred North Whitehead

To be a *Wow!* you have to be daring. You have to be willing to put your ideas, your talents, and yourself out there. How many people laughed at the Wright brothers? How many mocked Benjamin Franklin, Thomas Edison, and Henry Ford? Talk to any celebrity, and you'll find out that he or she had to put up with a fair amount of criticism before the good reviews started rolling in.

Part Two: How to Be a *Wow!*

Jeff Allen, a very funny friend of mine, once told me that in the early years of his career, a comedy-club owner told him he would never make a living as a stand-up comedian. Instead of getting depressed and quitting the business, Jeff just looked at him and said, "Hey, thanks!"

The guy, caught a little off guard by the smile on Jeff's face, asked, "For what?"

Jeff answered, "Because anyone who has ever made it has that one person he can point to as the one who tried to discourage him. You're my guy!" By the way, the guy was wrong. Jeff is indeed making a living and more as a stand-up comedian.

To be a *Wow!* a person has to risk being criticized, discouraged, laughed at, and unfairly treated by those who are either jealous or just miserable with their own lives.

You can't hit a home run from the bench. You have to step up to the plate, no matter how many people are or are not cheering, and you have to hit the ball and then cross your fingers and hope for the best. At the end of the day, win or lose, at least you know you were in the game.

Erma Bombeck once said that when she got to the end of her life, she wanted to be able to tell God that she had used everything He gave her. I believe she did. But there's no telling how much unused talent gets buried in graveyards, in perfect condition, never used, barely even unwrapped. These are people with incredible gifts that were just too timid to use them.

You miss 100 percent of the shots
you never take.

Wayne Gretzky

Twenty years from now you will be more
disappointed by the things you didn't do
than by the ones you did.
So throw off the bowlines.
Sail away from the safe harbor.
Catch the trade winds in your sails. Explore.
Dream. Discover.

Mark Twain

If you want to succeed, you should strike out on
new paths rather than travel the worn paths of
accepted success.

John D. Rockefeller

Part Two: How to Be a *Wow!*

You gain strength, courage, and confidence by every experience in which you really stop to look fear in the face. You are able to say to yourself, "I have lived through this horror. I can take the next thing that comes along." You must do the thing you think you cannot do.

Eleanor Roosevelt

Picture It!

Wow! = Vision

> The secret of achievement is to hold a picture of a successful outcome in mind.

Norman Vincent Peale

Envision yourself doing all the things you instinctively know you can do. Carry yourself as though you already are who you know you can be. Many people who have achieved great things in life say that they always had the vision of what they wanted to accomplish. They just needed to find a way to make it a reality.

We have little control over much of our lives, but those core beliefs, those internal messages we send to ourselves, that inner passion that drives us—the vision of who we want to become and what we want to accomplish—is something we do control. We can rise above the doubts, the naysayers, and even our circumstances.

Vision is the reason we hear heartwarming stories of people like Liz Murray. The daughter of two drug-addicted parents (one with a mental disease), fifteen-year-old Liz found herself all alone and having to survive life on the streets. But instead of giving up or becoming bitter or declaring that life owed her something, she pulled herself up from homelessness and put herself through Harvard. She had vision—she believed she could achieve her dream. And that's what makes the difference between ordinary and *Wow!*

Wows! don't settle for less than what they know they were created to accomplish.

The Creator has not given you a longing to do that which you have no ability to do.

Orison Swett Marden

"I know the plans I have for you,"
declares the LORD, "plans to prosper you
and not to harm you, plans to
give you hope and a future."

Jeremiah 29:11

Every man takes the limits
of his own field of vision
for the limits of the world.

Arthur Schopenhauer

Vision is the art of seeing things invisible.

Jonathan Swift

Don't Quit!

Wow! = Fortitude

Even a mistake may turn out to be the one thing
necessary to a worthwhile achievement.

Henry Ford

Mistakes. Discouragement. Failures. If you're going to do just about anything worthwhile in life, you're going to meet with some opposition. Sometimes it's other people, sometimes it's circumstances, and sometimes it's ourselves.

Fortitude is a mark of a *Wow!* person. It takes fortitude to keep going when the going gets tough. It takes fortitude to fail and go right back in there and try again, this time maybe in a different way. Fortitude enables us to see our mistakes as a training ground. Only with fortitude can we pull ourselves out of discouragement and say, "I'm not going to give up! I'm going to keep going until my vision becomes a reality."

Success is relative. It is what we can make of
the mess we have made of things.

T. S. Eliot

Troubles are often the tools by which
God fashions us for better things.

Henry Ward Beecher

Many of life's failures are people
who did not realize how close they were
to success when they gave up.

Thomas Edison

Do not quit! Hundreds of times I have watched
people throw in the towel at the one-yard line
while someone else comes along and makes a
fortune by just going that extra yard.

E. Joseph Cossman

Part Two: How to Be a *Wow!*

The road to success
is dotted with many
tempting parking places.

Unknown

One ship drives east and another drives west
With the selfsame winds that blow.
'Tis the set of the sails
And not the gales
That decides the way to go.

Ella Wheeler Wilcox

Get to Work!

Wow! = Sweat

> Opportunity is missed by most people because it is dressed in overalls and looks like work.

Thomas Edison

Do you realize how much could be accomplished if we only had the energy? There's no telling how far we could go.

Brains? Sure we need some intelligence, but we don't have to be geniuses. Many of the most successful people in the world were poor students.

Breaks? They help, but if we don't have the talent or the skills, a break won't do us much good.

Brawn isn't a requirement either. Just look at how much Mother Teresa accomplished.

But energy? Sweat? Hard work? Now there's something that's a requirement. We can't be a *Wow!* unless we're willing to sweat a little.

Part Two: How to Be a *Wow!*

The world belongs to the energetic.

Ralph Waldo Emerson

The reason so many people never get anywhere
in life is because when opportunity knocks, they
are out in the backyard
looking for four-leaf clovers.

Walter Chrysler

If we wait for the moment when everything,
absolutely everything is ready,
we shall never begin.

Ivan Turgenev

Dream It!

Wow! = Dreams

Far away there in the sunshine are my highest
aspirations. I may not reach them,
but I can look up and see their beauty, believe in
them, and try to follow where they lead.

Louisa May Alcott

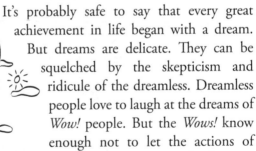

It's probably safe to say that every great achievement in life began with a dream. But dreams are delicate. They can be squelched by the skepticism and ridicule of the dreamless. Dreamless people love to laugh at the dreams of *Wow!* people. But the *Wows!* know enough not to let the actions of those people—the things usually done out of jealousy—discourage them from pursuing their dreams. They know that dealing with dream squelchers goes with the territory. Anytime we break ahead of the pack, others will be nipping at our heels. That's because our heels are the only things they can catch. They nip at what they can reach. But a little heel nipping won't hold back a *Wow!* You've proven that.

And even though you've accomplished what some said you couldn't, you don't gloat. That's another thing about *Wows!*—they have plenty of class as well as a healthy helping of humility.

All men who have achieved great things
have been great dreamers.

Orison Swett Marden

If you can dream it, you can do it.

Walt Disney

We grow great by dreams. All big men are dreamers. . . . Some of us let these great dreams die, but others nourish and protect them; nurse them through bad days till they bring them to the sunshine and light which comes always to those who sincerely hope that their dreams will come true.

Woodrow Wilson

Part Two: How to Be a *Wow!*

When you dare to dream, dare to follow that
dream, dare to suffer through the pain, sacrifice,
self-doubts, and friction from the world,
you will genuinely impress yourself.

Laura Schlessinger

Dreams are the touchstones of our character.

Henry David Thoreau

To fulfill a dream, to be allowed to sweat over
lonely labor, to be given a chance to create,
is the meat and potatoes of life.
The money is the gravy.

Bette Davis

Dreams are renewable. No matter what our age
or condition, there are still untapped possibilities
within us and new beauty waiting to be born.

Dale E. Turner

You're the only one who can make the
difference. Whatever your dream is, go for it.

Earvin "Magic" Johnson

Part Two: How to Be a *Wow!*

The future belongs to those
who believe in the beauty of their dreams.

Eleanor Roosevelt

I'm a Believer!

Wow! = Faith

A pessimist sees the difficulty in every opportunity; an optimist sees the opportunity in every difficulty.

Winston Churchill

Faith is the force that keeps us going. It keeps us believing we'll eventually succeed, even after failing again and again. It's that internal voice that sort of giggles when naysayers tell us to give up. Faith isn't merely hoping we'll succeed; it's being convinced that no matter what comes our way, we can't help but succeed. It may not be today. Or even tomorrow. But one day our dreams will become reality.

Faith in ourselves, in our God-ordained purpose, in our visions, and in our dreams is an important part of being a *Wow!*

Part Two: How to Be a *Wow!*

If you hear a voice within you say
"you cannot paint," then by all means paint,
and that voice will be silenced.

Vincent van Gogh

Faith is to believe what we do not see; and the
reward of this faith is to see what we believe.

Saint Augustine of Hippo

Have faith and pursue the unknown end.

Oliver Wendell Holmes

One can never consent to creep
when one feels an impulse to soar.

Helen Keller

All the Way!

Wow! = Dedication

Don't be afraid to give your best to what seemingly are small jobs. Every time you conquer one it makes you that much stronger. If you do the little jobs well, the big ones will tend to take care of themselves.

Dale Carnegie

Give it everything you've got. Don't wait until your boss increases your paycheck to start giving better service to the customers. Let your paycheck catch up to your service. Always give more than what is required or expected of you. Be someone others notice and remember when promotions or raises come due. Be the name that comes up when people think of faithfulness and attention to duty. Dedication—it's almost impossible to be a *Wow!* without it.

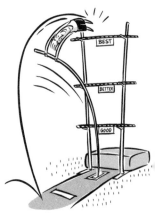

Whatever you are, be a good one.

Abraham Lincoln

Almost always, the creative dedicated minority
has made the world better.

Martin Luther King Jr.

Life means to have something definite to do—a
mission to fulfill—and in the measure in which
we avoid setting our life to something, we make
it empty. Human life, by its very nature, has to
be dedicated to something.

Jose Ortega y Gasset

Be Ready!

Wow! = Preparation

Winning is the science of being totally prepared.

Gracie Allen

When opportunity knocks, we don't just have to answer the door, we have to be dressed and ready to greet whatever's on the other side. But many of us get caught in our bathrobes, with a jammed door, having to peer through the window and wave for opportunity to come back at a more opportune time and give us another chance. It rarely does.

Being ready for opportunity means being prepared. We need to hone our skills, increase our knowledge, practice and practice our craft, learn from our failures . . . and somehow be dressed and ready to go. Preparation is another important part of being a *Wow!*

To stay ahead, you must have your next idea waiting in the wings.

Rosabeth Moss Kanter

Failure to prepare is preparing to fail.

John Wooden

Part Two: How to Be a *Wow!*

Luck is what happens
when preparation meets opportunity.

Seneca

You better live your best and act your best
and think your best today; for today is the sure
preparation for tomorrow and all the other
tomorrows that follow.

Harriet Martineau

Tune It Out!

Wow! = Selective Listening

Pay as little attention to discouragement as possible. Plough ahead as a steamer does, rough or smooth—rain or shine. To carry your cargo and make your port is the point.

Maltbie Davenport Babcock

On your way to this proud moment, you've no doubt run across your share of naysayers. They're the uninvited guests who come into our days (often when we are already feeling discouraged) and insist on telling us their negative opinions.

But a *Wow!* has learned to listen selectively. Do pay attention to those who encourage you, who truly love you and want what's best for you, those who are proud of you and believe you can achieve all you were meant to achieve. As for the others, buy a good set of earplugs.

It's simply a matter of doing what you do best
and not worrying about
what the other fellow is going to do.

John R. Amos

What we do not see, what most of us never
suspect of existing, is the silent but irresistible
power which comes to the rescue of those who
fight on in the face of discouragement.

Napoleon Hill

Let no feeling of discouragement prey upon you,
and in the end you are sure to succeed.

Abraham Lincoln

Be You!

Wow! = Self-Awareness

Men go abroad to wonder at the heights of mountains, at the huge waves of the sea, at the long courses of the rivers, at the vast compass of the ocean, at the circular motions of the stars, and they pass by themselves without wondering.

St. Augustine

The world has enough imitators. One look at an Elvis-impersonator reunion will tell you that. I was a fan of Elvis, and I even enjoy some of the impersonators. But if all you do is copy others, no matter how well you do it, you are cheating the world out of seeing another gifted person—you! So don't get trapped in the comfort of following someone else's tried-and-true method or dream. You have your own path to follow. You have your own talents to give to the world. So be yourself. Be the best you possible. Be the you the world is ready to see.

If a man does not keep pace with his companions, perhaps it is because he hears a different drummer. Let him step to the music which he hears, however measured or far away.

Henry David Thoreau

Part Two: How to Be a *Wow!*

Every man's work, whether it be literature or music or pictures or architecture or anything else, is always a portrait of himself.

Samuel Butler

Trust yourself. Create the kind of self that you will be happy to live with all your life. Make the most of yourself by fanning the tiny, inner sparks of possibility into flames of achievement.

Foster C. McClellan

We must overcome the notion that we must be regular . . . it robs you of the chance to be extraordinary and leads you to the mediocre.

Uta Hagen

It takes courage to grow up
and become who you really are.

E. E. Cummings

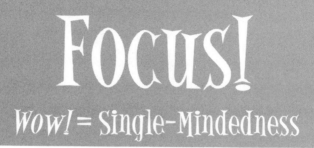

FOCUS!

Wow! = Single-Mindedness

To be successful, you must decide exactly
what you want to accomplish,
then resolve to pay the price to get it.

Nelson Bunker Hunt

A successful person may have hundreds of ideas. But
there comes a time when we have to focus on each one
individually. Single-mindedness is an important part of
seeing a project through to the end. How many build-
ing plans, canvases, books, movies, and inventions are

sitting half finished in someone's desk drawer or locked in a computer? Being single-minded and finishing what we start is a prerequisite for being a *Wow!* To compete, we have to complete.

When I was first starting out in the comedy writing business, I made up a "To-Do" list of things that needed to be attended to in order to advance my embryonic career. Of course, there were things I would rather do first, like watch a game on TV or go to a movie. So I wrote a little reminder at the top of each page. It read, "In order to achieve what you love, sometimes you have to sacrifice what you like."

Gene Perret

The person who makes a success of living
is the one who sees his goal steadily
and aims for it unswervingly.

Cecil B. DeMille

Part Two: How to Be a *Wow!*

We succeed only as we identify in life,
or in war, or in anything else,
a single overriding objective, and make all other
considerations bend to that one objective.

Dwight D. Eisenhower

A leader, once convinced that a particular course
of action is the right one, must . . . be undaunted
when the going gets tough.

Ronald Reagan

Love It!

Wow! = Passion

There is always one moment in childhood when the door opens and lets the future in.

Graham Greene

I am convinced there is a passion that lies within each one of us that was placed there by God. Unfortunately, some of us have buried it so deeply under pain and worry and fear and time constraints that we barely feel it anymore. Even though it may be dormant, it's still there. That's the one thing about true passion: we can ignore it, but it won't go away. It may take a backseat to everything else in our lives, but it doesn't disappear. It sits silently in the corners of our souls waiting for its chance to rise up. But it won't force its way to the forefront of our calendars. It waits to be invited. It wants to be pursued. We have to choose to follow our passions. Otherwise, we choose not to follow it.

Wow! people have the courage to do what they love and to live their passion.

Just don't give up trying to do what you really want to do. Where there's love and inspiration, I don't think you can go wrong.

Ella Fitzgerald

My passions were all gathered together like
fingers that made a fist.
Drive is considered aggression today;
I knew it then as purpose.

Bette Davis

Only passions, great passions,
can elevate the soul to great things.

Denis Diderot

Get Over It!

Wow! = Letting Go

Stop the mindless wishing that things would
be different. Rather than wasting time and
emotional and spiritual energy in explaining why
we don't have what we want, we can start to
pursue other ways to get it.

Greg Anderson

It's hard to let go. Especially when we've grown so
accustomed to carrying everything around with us.
We carry our problems (and sometimes, unnecessarily,
the problems of others too). We carry our own faults and

failures, and sometimes the blame for other people's faults and failures as well. No wonder there's so much stress in our lives! We've overburdened ourselves. It's great to help others, but sometimes in our helping, we go too far and end up stunting those people's personal growth and hindering ours.

Wows! have healthy boundaries.

It's also important to know when to let go of baggage. Carrying around too many old wounds and problems will only slow us down.

Wow! people know how to pack lightly.

Some people believe that holding on and
hanging in there are signs of great strength.
However, there are times when it takes
much more strength to know when
to let go—and then do it.

Ann Landers

Part Two: How to Be a *Wow!*

! ! !

○ ● ○

Life is a process of becoming, a combination of
states we have to go through. Where people fail
is that they wish to elect a state and remain in it.
This is a kind of death.

Anais Nin

The marksman hitteth the target partly by pulling,
partly by letting go.

Egyptian Proverb

They who plough the sea do not carry
the winds in their hands.

Publius Syrus

Be Your Best!

Wow! = Building a Better Tomorrow

How wonderful it is that nobody need
wait a single moment before
starting to improve the world.

Anne Frank

Wow! people make a difference in the world by being the best they can be. Their inventions, discoveries, arts, inspiration, and dedicated service make life better for everyone.

It's easy to gripe about the transportation workers creating traffic jams and generally messing up our lives, but once the new highway is completed, we wonder how we ever managed without it. It's easy to complain about the long wait in the emergency room, but if it weren't for the dedicated staff, where would we go when we get hurt and need immediate medical care?

If not for the vision and dedication of *Wow!* people, we wouldn't have many of the things we enjoy and have come to rely on in our communities and homes.

Wow! people believe they can improve life—and they do it.

The secret of success is constancy to purpose.

Benjamin Disraeli

I have one life and one chance to make it count for something. . . . I'm free to choose what that something is, and the something I've chosen is my faith. Now, my faith goes beyond theology and religion and requires considerable work and effort. My faith demands—this is not optional—my faith demands that I do whatever I can, wherever I am, whenever I can, for as long as I can with whatever I have to try to make a difference.

Jimmy Carter

It's easy to make a buck. It's a lot tougher to make a difference.

Tom Brokaw

Part Two: How to Be a *Wow!*

Be courageous.
Be disciplined.
Be unique.
Be willing.
Be available.
Be encouraged.
Be the best you can be.
Be a *Wow!*

A Wow! is someone
who shows up, does the work,
doesn't quit, and always does
his or her best. That is you!

In our book
you are a
WOW!